City Shapes

Rectangles

By Jennifer S. Burke

Welcome Books

SCHOLASTIC INC.

New York Toronto London Auckland Sydney
Mexico City New Delhi Hong Kong Buenos Aires

Photo Credits: Cover photo © by PhotoDisc/Getty Images.
Interior photos © by Indexstock.
Contributing Editors: Mark Beyer and Eliza Berkowitz
Book Design: Michael DeLisio

ISBN 0-516-24183-4

12 11 10 9 8 7 6 5 4 3 2   2 3 4 5 6 7/0

Printed in the U.S.A.   10

First Scholastic printing, September 2002

Contents

1 Rectangles in the Dark   4

2 Rectangles on a Building   10

3 Looking Through Rectangles   14

4 Rectangles in the Park   18

5 New Words   22

6 Index   23

7 About the Author   23

The city is getting dark.

Signs light up.

Can you find the **bright** rectangle signs?

5

It is winter in the city.

There is **snow** on the ground.

Can you count the rectangles in the fence?

Summer in the city is hot.

The **building** has a pool on the **roof**.

In the summer, you can cool off in the pool.

The pool is a rectangle.

9

Look up!

The building is covered in rectangles.

Can you find any other rectangles?

11

The buildings are in the shape of rectangles.

Some are big and some are small.

Which building is the biggest rectangle?

13

You can see through some rectangles.

There are many rectangles here.

Each window is a rectangle.

15

The **museum** building has many rectangle shapes.

How many different-size rectangles do you see?

16

17

The park is a good place to find rectangles.

Sometimes you can climb on rectangles.

Which rectangles are for climbing?

You can find rectangles by themselves or with other rectangles.

Some rectangles are big and some are small.

It is fun to find rectangle shapes in the city.

New Words

bright (**bryt**) lit up by light

building (**bil**-ding) lit up by light

museum (myoo-**zee**-um) a
building that has art or history
objects

roof (**roof**) the top of a building

snow (**snoh**) water that freezes
in the air

Index

bright, 4
building, 8, 10, 12,
   16

museum, 16

park, 18

roof, 8

snow, 6

window, 14

About the Author
Jennifer S. Burke is a teacher and a writer living in New York City. She holds a master's degree in reading education from Queens College, New York.

Reading Consultants
Kris Flynn, Coordinator, Small School District Literacy, The San Diego County Office of Education

Shelly Forys, Certified Reading Recovery Specialist, W.J. Zahnow Elementary School, Waterloo, IL

Peggy McNamara, Professor, Bank Street College of Education, Reading and Literacy Program